Rule of Thumb

A Guide to Small Business Basics

Marian Shalander Kaiser and Michael Mitilier

Published by

WriteLife
(An imprint of Boutique of
Quality Books Publishing
Company)

www.writelife.com

Rule of Thumb

www.ruleofthumbbiz.com

Printed in the United States of America

ISBN 978-1-60808-024-3 (p)
ISBN 978-1-60808-085-4 (e)

First Edition

Contents

Why Rule of Thumb?

This book is part of the Rule of Thumb series produced in affiliation with the Rule of Thumb for Business whose mission is to "enrich business growth and development." The Rule of Thumb series offers basic information in plain language that will help you start, grow and sustain your business. The explanation for using the *"rule of thumb"* concept was introduced in the first book and is included again here.

Throughout history, a *"rule of thumb"* was used in measurements in a wide variety of businesses and vocations. The following list gives a few examples of how the thumb was used for measuring:

- In agriculture, the thumb was used to measure the depth at which to plant a seed.
- In restaurants and pubs, the thumb was used to measure the temperature of beer and ale.
- Tailors used the thumb to make sure enough space was allowed between the person's skin and his/her clothing. For example, the space between the cuff of the sleeve and the wrist had to be at least the width of the thumb.

- Carpenters used the width of the thumb rather than a ruler for measuring. For example, a notch in a board may need to be cut two thumb widths from the edge.

A *"rule of thumb"* is an idea or rule that may be applied in most situations, but not all. The *"rules of thumb"* in this book give you many reliable, convenient and simple rules that will help you remember many "dos" and "don'ts" that go with owning and running a business. Many of these concepts can also be used in a variety of business situations ranging from management, sales, customer service, human resources and leadership. The information is designed to be easy, simple and action-oriented. To learn more about the Rule of Thumb for Business organization visit our website at www.ruleofthumbbiz.com. – *Rule of Thumb for Business.*

Introduction
What's in it (this book) for me?

A business owner needs to be aware of legal requirements, financial resources, record-keeping requirements, ways to market a business, communication skills, human resource laws, as well as issues that may arise on a day-to-day basis. Being aware of and following regulations and laws help you be sure that your business is meeting all legal requirements. Having the knowledge and skills needed to run your business on a day to-day basis increases the odds of your success.

This book answers many questions you may have about starting and running a business. The major topics discussed in this book include the following:

- What steps do I need to take to start a business?
- Do I know the differences among a sole proprietorship, an s-corp, a partnership, etc? How will I know which one is the best for me?
- What do I need to know about finances and bookkeeping?
- What other records do I need to keep?

- Will I need to use technology in my business? How will I know what technology my business needs?
- What administration and management skills will I need?
- How important are communication skills to my business? How can I improve my communication skills?
- How will I advertise and promote my business?
- What information must I have to manage human resources?

Using the information in this book will help you set up a business and be on your way to running it successfully.

Chapter 1
Starting a Business:
What steps do I need to take?

Starting a business takes careful planning. Awareness of legal requirements and the basic steps needed to establish a business will help you plan the start-up process and stay organized. Information about various business structures and legal issues are extremely helpful. When in doubt, consult your Secretary of State's office or a lawyer for accurate information.

<u>What are the basic steps I must take
to set up a business?</u>

The following steps will help you plan what you need to do to get started:

- Learn about other businesses that do what you plan to do in your business.
- Plan your business (size, number of employees, etc.).
- Get needed business assistance and training.
- Choose a location for your business.
- Secure financing for your business.

- Decide on which legal structure is best for your business (detailed in following section).
- Register the business name with your state (Secretary of State Office in most cases).
- Obtain a Federal Tax ID number, also called an Employee Identification Number (EIN), by going to the Internal Revenue Service website (irs.gov) for information on applying online, by phone or by fax.
- Register with state and local departments of revenue.
- Get required business licenses and permits.
- Learn about employer legal responsibilities.

Rule of Thumb:
When in doubt, ask a professional.

What business structure should I choose?

The business structure you choose needs to fit the type and size of business you will be running. Ask for help if you are not sure which structure is best for you. A tax expert or lawyer is often a good source of advice on this issue.

The following list gives information about each business structure:

Sole Proprietorship: This business structure has one owner who is legally responsible (liable) for all the business's debts and obligations. The *easiest* and most common way to structure your business is the sole proprietorship. In most cases, the owner is responsible for the day-to-day operation of business. A sole proprietor owns all business assets (building, furnishing, electronic equipment, inventory, vehicles, etc.) and profits. *He or she also has total responsibility for business liabilities and debts.* Sole proprietorships are found in all business areas. This type of business may be a full-time or part-time business, a one-person operation, a business with many employees, a home-based business, an online business, or a traditional store-front or office business.

Partnership: This business structure is one business with two or more people owning it. In general, each partner contributes to all areas of the business, including labor and skill, expertise, money, and property. Each partner also shares in the business's profits and losses.

Because decision-making in a partnership includes all partners, openly discussing all business-related issues from the beginning and establishing a legal partnership are extremely important. The legal partnership/agreement should describe how business decisions will be made, how profits will be divided, how disputes will be resolved, how change in ownership will be handled (bringing in new partners or buying out current partners), and how the partnership will be dissolved if the partners agree to dissolve it. While not legally required, written partnership agreements are strongly recommended. Running a business partnership without a legal agreement could be risky because of differing opinions of the partners.

Corporation (C Corp): This business structure is a legal entity owned by many people or groups called shareholders. A shareholder may purchase shares in the business. The business decides how many shares will be available for people or groups to purchase and what the initial cost per share will be. Most small businesses that choose to sell shares start with 1,000 shares, but they may choose to issue more or fewer shares. As an independent legal entity, the corporation itself, not the shareholders who own shares, is legally responsible for the actions and debts of the business.

Corporations are more complex than other business structures. Corporations have higher administrative costs, and the legal and tax requirements are also more complex. Corporations must pay taxes as an entity separate from its shareholders. Additionally, the dividends (earnings on shares owned) earned by shareholders are also taxed on their individual income tax returns. Corporations are usually recommended for larger, well-established companies with multiple employees because the complex legal and tax issues are too costly for small businesses.

Businesses that choose to use the corporation structure may sell ownership shares in the business through stock offerings. Offering stock is referred to as "going public." The initial public offering (IPO) is a major selling point for attracting investment money and high quality employees.

Limited Liability Company (LLC): An LLC has some features of a corporation and some features of a partnership. It provides limited liability (legal responsibility) for partners, as does a corporation, but also allows the tax advantages and operating flexibility of a partnership.

The "owners" of an LLC are referred to as "members." Laws vary from state to state, but in general the members may be a single individual (one owner), two or more people, corporations, other LLCs, and other legal entities.

LLCs are not taxed as separate businesses apart from the members/owners. Corporations *are* taxed separately from the stockholders. All profits and losses are "passed through" the business to each LLC member. For example, if a member owns a 25% interest in the LLC, he/she receives 25% of the profits or losses. Members must report these profits and losses on their personal federal tax returns, the same as the owners of a partnership would do.

Sub S Corporation: An S Corporation (or S Corp) is a special type of corporation created by electing to file as an S Corp on the federal tax return. This election allows the business to receive Subchapter S designation from the Internal Revenue Service (IRS). By electing to file as an S Corp, a domestic corporation avoids double taxation of the C Corporation (both to the corporation and to the shareholders).

Before one may elect to file his/her businesses as an S Corp, the business must first be chartered as a corporation in the state where it is headquartered. According to the IRS, S Corporations are "considered by law to be a unique entity, separate and apart from those who own it." An S Corp provides a limit on the legal financial responsibility of the owner ("shareholder"). Even with this limitation, the financial protection is limited: S Corps do not always shield owners from all law suits, such as one filed for a workplace accident.

The difference between an S Corp and a traditional corporation (C Corp) is that the S Corp passes profits and losses to the shareholders' personal tax returns.

The business itself is not taxed, only the shareholders. Please note one important fact of which to be aware: Any shareholder who works for the company must pay himself or herself "reasonable compensation." Reasonable compensation means that any shareholder working for the S Corp must be paid fair market value for his or her work, or the IRS may reclassify any additional corporate earnings as "wages."

Nonprofit: A nonprofit organization (NPO) is a business for which making a profit is NOT its primary purpose. Nonprofits provide programs and services for charitable, educational, religious, or artistic activities for public or private causes. A nonprofit organization is prohibited from distributing profits to the organization's directors, officers, employees, or members. Any income of the nonprofit must go back into the organization. Nonprofits, though, may hire and pay staff to carry out operational and administrative functions.

A nonprofit organization incorporates as a 501(c) corporation and may choose from 26 types – 501(c)(1) to 501(c)(26). Section 501(c)(3), the most common federal tax exemption for nonprofits, exempts the nonprofit from paying taxes on income directly related to the organization's mission. Many nonprofits are most often simply referred to as 501(c)(3) corporations.

Rule of Thumb:
Know what your goals are. Avoid running your business by the seat of your pants.

What are the benefits and drawbacks of the various types of business structures?

The following table lists the most common benefits and drawbacks of the types of business structures:

	Benefits	Drawbacks
Sole Proprietorship	Easy and inexpensive Owner controls all aspects of the business – eliminates disagreements All income goes to owner to keep or reinvest	Owner is legally responsible for all financial and other obligations More difficult to raise money for the business Less attractive to prospective employees
Partnership	Easy and inexpensive Financial risk shared by more than one person Often brings multiple skills and knowledge to the business Advantage in hiring employees by offering partnership share in the business (if owners choose to offer this benefit)	Legal responsibilities (financial and otherwise) fall to all partners Disagreements among partners can cause disputes that affect the business Profits must be shared by all partners

Corporation	Limited legal responsibility of shareholders Ability to raise investment dollars Taxes filed separately from shareholders Attractive to employees – generally offers benefits along with salaries	Time-consuming to start and to operate Costs: start-up, operating and taxes Double taxing: corporation is taxed, and the shareholders are taxed on dividends Great deal of additional paperwork because of state and federal regulations
LLC	Members protected from personal legal responsibility (law suits brought against the LLC, not its partners) Less record-keeping required than for C Corp Smaller start-up costs Fewer restrictions on sharing profits No double taxing: LLC is not taxed itself; profits are reported by partners on individual tax returns	Limited life: in some states the business must be dissolved if one or more members leave (check with your Secretary of State's office) Self-employment taxes: members of LLCs are considered self-employed and must contribute to Medicare and Social Security

S Corp	Tax savings: S Corp itself not taxed; profits or losses shown by corporation are reported on the shareholders' tax returns Business expenses are eligible for tax deductions and credits Business has independent life separate from shareholders	Stricter operational process (directors and shareholders must have meetings and minutes) Shareholder must receive reasonable compensation for work performed
Nonprofit	Tax exempt Eligible for grants and donations (tax deductible by the donor) Encourages tax-deductible donations to the organization Limited personal liability Eligible discounts (postage, advertising rates, free air time for public service announcements)	Many government requirements Requires detailed bookkeeping Taxes on unrelated activities No financial compensation for board of directors If organization is dissolved, all assets must go to other nonprofits

What steps do I need to take to get the business officially registered with the state?

- Decide on the best legal structure for your business.
- Register your business name with the Secretary of State's office.

- In many states, the default name is the name of the business owner. You may use dba ("doing business as") followed by a business name.
- Depending on the type of business structure and your state's laws, you may register a name of your choice (check with your Secretary of State's office).

- Get a federal tax identification number (especially if you have employees).
- Register with your state department of revenue.
- Obtain all required state and local business licenses and/or permits that are specific to your industry. For example, a restaurant must have a permit from the state department of health.

What other issues do I need to think about to get the business upand running?

Articles of Incorporation (also called "Certificate of Incorporation" or "Corporate Charter") form a document that sets out the main rules that explain in detail how the business or corporation is managed. Articles are filed with the Secretary of State's office, typically for the following types of business structures:

- C Corp
- S Corp
- Nonprofit

Bylaws constitute a document that defines how the business is organized, the business structure, and procedures for how the organization should be run. For example, bylaws may define how many people are on the board of directors, how many years they may serve, how they are elected, how they may be removed, etc. A for profit business may choose to have bylaws or not. Nonprofit organizations are required to have bylaws. Bylaws typically include the following:

- Name of organization
- Purpose of the organization
- Members of the board of directors
- Officers of the board of directors
- Meetings – how often and who must be present
- Committees
- Who is eligible to vote

Examples of bylaws may be found in many places on the Internet by searching for "bylaws template."

Mission Statement is a short statement (usually one or two sentences) that defines what your business does and whom it serves. It guides the overall actions and provides a sense of direction for the organization. For instance, if you run a clothing store for women, ask yourself what type of merchandise you carry and who will be the most likely buyer of this clothing? For-profit businesses may choose to have a mission statement or not. Nonprofit organizations must have mission statements.

Hiring a lawyer to complete the paper work and filings may be a good decision. A lawyer will tell you what you need to do to comply with regulations and laws to make sure that nothing is left out. Having a knowledgeable lawyer may save you a great deal of time and money later on.

> **Rule of Thumb:**
> Make sure you have filed all the legal documents needed for your business. Keep copies in your business files.

Where do I go if I need help?

- University business colleges
- Law schools
- SBA (Small Business Administration) Website (sba.gov)
- SCORE (Service Corps of Retired Executives)
- Business.usa.gov
- ROTB (Rule of Thumb for Business) website (ruleofthumbbiz.com)
- Internal Revenue Service (irs.gov)

Legal Issues

Be sure to check with a lawyer or your Secretary of State's office to make sure that your business is legally registered and that you are following all laws, rules and regulations. Consulting a tax professional will also help you keep all your finances and record-keeping legal. The Internal Revenue Service will not hesitate to fine you if you are reporting income and expenses incorrectly.

Chapter 2
Finances: How do I deal with them?

Keeping track of your business's finances is crucial to your business success. You cannot know where your business stands if you don't follow the money. Knowing the financial situation of your business is critical for making decisions. You also must keep accurate records for income tax purposes.

What's the one most important thing I need to remember?

NEVER, NEVER, NEVER mix your business money with your personal money. It's easy to do, but don't do it! Keep a separate bank account only for your business. If the IRS should happen to audit your business tax returns, business money mingled with personal money could create many problems and result in fines.

Rule of Thumb:
Always keep business money and records separate from your personal money and records. Set up a separate bank account for your business.

What are some basics I need to remember?

- Pay yourself a salary. You are an employee of the company, even if you own it.
- Keep careful records of all money received and what it is for.
- Make sure your receipts and bank deposits match exactly.
- Keep careful records of all expenses:
  - Record what each bill is for.
  - Record when each is paid, along with the check number with which it was paid. You might also consider keeping a photocopy of the check.
- Decide if you will track finances manually or with computer software.
  - Tracking manually often works well for extremely small businesses.
  - A business with more than one employee may want to track finances with bookkeeping software. Check out several bookkeeping software programs to find the best fit for your needs. Avoid paying several thousand dollars for a program when a $300 program more than meets your needs.
- Decide how you will accept payment from your customers.

Cash: Some businesses operate on a cash-only basis because of fraud issues with checks and credit cards. Advances in technology require business owners to ask if limiting payment options is hurting the business.

Check: Additional expenses for credit and debit cards may not be cost effective for your business. Be sure to have a detailed check acceptance policy to help identify the customer and avoid bad checks.

Online payment: Decide if providing an online system for payment is cost-effective for your business. Remember that most online payments are made with credit or debit cards, which will have fees for the business attached to them.

Extension of credit to customers through invoices: This practice is common in some industries, especially service industries. Be sure that you understand the risk involved. Establish a detailed credit policy before you extend credit. Make sure you understand consumer protection laws to protect yourself and your business.

What State and Federal (IRS) issues do I have to keep in mind?

- Withholding for income taxes
- Withholding for Social Security and Medicare taxes
- Due dates for payments to IRS
- Other IRS laws/rules/regulations
- State sales tax on goods or services: be sure to check with your state laws

Audit requirements – check with your tax professional to find out if you must conduct annual audits or financial reviews. Financial reviews check to see if you are meeting all requirements and standards for your business. An audit is a detailed review of all finances for the business, including hard assets like equipment and buildings.

Rule of Thumb:
Pay yourself a salary. You are an employee of your company.

What types of taxes may affect my business?

Income tax: This tax is assessed on earnings. It must be paid as you earn or receive income during the year. For most individual workers, this tax is paid through withholding from one's paycheck. Businesses must also make income tax payments throughout the year.

Estimated tax: This method of paying income tax is used in certain situations instead of regular withholding from paychecks. It is most often paid quarterly. This method of payment is common for businesses.

Self-employment tax: If you are self-employed (e.g., the owner of a sole proprietorship), this tax covers Social Security and Medicare.

Employment tax: This tax is required for all

businesses that have employees. It covers Social Security and Medicare taxes, federal income tax, and federal unemployment tax.

Excise tax: This tax covers special taxes on goods and services specified in the IRS tax code. For instance, fuel taxes, communication taxes, hotel/motel taxes are defined as excise taxes. Check with your tax professional to determine if you must collect an excise tax and how much that tax is.

What do I need for filing a business income tax return? (And, YES, you MUST file a return.)

Consider hiring a tax professional to make sure you are meeting all legal requirements. Do some research before you hire someone. Ask him/her to provide the names of clients who may give you recommendations for this person. Some people may believe the cost for hiring a tax professional is high. But compared to penalties and fines that you may face if you don't know the tax laws, the professional fees are not so bad. Pay attention to deadlines. The IRS will assess penalties and fines for late payments.

Audit requirements: Again, check with your tax professional to determine what requirements may or may not exist for your business regarding audits or reviews.

Rule of Thumb:
Consult a tax professional.

What can I deduct as business expense?

The most common deductible business expenses include the following:

- Salaries
- Benefits (be aware that not all benefits are deductible)
- Space rental or purchase
- Utilities and phone
- Office supplies
- Postage
- Internet access fees
- Start-up costs
- Marketing and public relations
- Depreciation (office furniture, buildings, machinery,   equipment)
- Business use of home (if you have a home office); rules and regulations apply – check with your tax professional
- Car and truck expenses

Keep in mind that the above list is not complete. Track ALL expenses and check with your tax professional for information regarding what is and what is not deductible.

A deductible expense must be both ordinary and

necessary. An ordinary expense is one that is common and accepted in your field of business, trade or profession. A necessary expense is one that is helpful or appropriate for your field of business, trade or profession.

Some people mistakenly think these items are deductible – they are not:

- Personal parties (as opposed to office parties)
- Mileage on your vehicle for personal use
- Non-business cell phones or computers

Why do I need to keep records?

Every business MUST keep records. Good records will help you with the following:

- Monitor the progress of your business
- Provide accurate information to prepare financial statements
- Identify sources of income
- Keep accurate records of deductible expenses
- Supply necessary information to prepare your tax return
- Provide a paper trail for items reported on your tax return (such as the purchase of a computer and other expenses)

What is my credit score, and why is it important?

Many people think that their personal credit score has nothing to do with their business. Wrong! Your personal credit score is vital to getting a loan or other funding for your business.

A credit score is required if you apply for a business loan, whether for a start-up business or one that has been in operation for many years. This credit report is a detailed listing of your credit history, (e.g., payments to credit cards, car loans, home loanes, etc.).

Banks will check your PERSONAL credit score. The reasoning behind this action is that if you are unable to handle your personal finances, how are you expected to handle business finances?

- Ranges for credit scores (highest possible score is 830)
  - 726-830: Low Risk
  - 700-725: Medium - Low Risk
  - 626-699: Medium Risk
  - 351-625: Medium - High Risk
  - 330-350: High Risk
- Finding your credit score
  - Experian
  - Equifax
  - TransUnion

You may access your credit at any time, but each one of these credit report companies allows a once-a-year free access to your credit score

> **Rule of Thumb:**
> Always know your credit score.

What do I need when applying for a business loan?

Before deciding to apply for a loan, you should consider various options from micro-lending to angel investors, as well as banks. But no matter who your lender is, you will need to have specific information available to that lender.

- What to ask yourself if you are considering asking for a business loan
  - Why am I applying for this loan - Do I truly need the loan?

- How will the loan be used?
- What assets need to be purchased with money from the loan?
- What other business debt do I have?
- Who are my creditors?
- Who are the members of my management team?

When you apply for a business loan, lenders will ask for personal background information such as address, other names used, criminal record (if any), places you have lived, and educational background. Your lender will obtain your credit report as part of the application process. The report purchased by lenders will include the credit score.

Have a clear, concise business financial statement or projection that includes the following:

- Profit and loss statements
- Bank statements
- Accounts receivable
- Accounts payable
- Collateral
- Legal documents (articles of incorporation, lease agreements, etc.)
- Start-up or expansion costs (if applicable)
- Cash flow estimates
- Sales figures/receipts
- Annual expenses

Remember that the lender will also consider your return on investment (ROI), which is how much profit you will make after your expenses are paid, including loan payments.

All loan programs require you to provide a sound written business plan. If you do not have a written business plan, go to sba.gov or business.usa.gov to find samples of business plans. If you need assistance preparing the business plan, consult the business college at a local university or community college. Most will provide assistance free of charge.

Legal Issues

Having accurate, detailed records is extremely important if you are audited by the IRS (Internal Revenue Sevice). Keeping personal finances and business finances totally separate will help you avoid legal problems with the IRS. It will also help you if you need to apply for a loan. Creditors do not look favorably upon mingled business and personal finances.

Protect yourself by making sure you have the necessary insurance policies, such as liability, fire and theft, workers' compensation, and disability.

As always, check with a professional to make sure that you are taking care of all legal issues properly. Understand that your creditors may sue you if you do not pay your bills.

Chapter 3
Technology: What do I need and why?

Technology can help you run your business more efficiently and effectively. Beware, though, of investing your hard-earned dollars into expensive technology that does not serve you well or that does far more than your business requires.

What are some technology tools that help small businesses?

While your business may not necessarily need all the following technology tools, they are generally useful in most small businesses.

Website: provides information to a wider audience and brings in potential customers

Anti-virus software: protects your computer equipment from viruses that may destroy your information (Most Internet service providers have anti-virus systems included in the purchase of the monthly service.)

Accounting software: keeping accurate financial records helps increase your business success

Google account: offers useful tools, products and services, many of which are free

File backup system: makes sure that your hard drive and your files are backed up, either through purchased hardware and/or software or by subscribing to an online backup service

Smart phone: allows you and your staff to be mobile, not tied to the office; allows you to complete transactions, stay in communication with staff and clients/customers and vendors, thereby increasing overall productivity

Laptop computer: allows you to be more productive during business travel and to give business presentations

Intranet: allows file sharing, editing, and communication to effectively manage projects with people inside your office

Conferencing tools: allows you to have meetings with people from various locations; can be accomplished through online services

Rule of Thumb:
Technology can make you more efficient.
If it doesn't, re-evaluate what you are
using and why.

What should I consider before deciding what technology to purchase?

- How big is my business?
  - How many employees will need to use computers and other technology?
  - How much information will need to be stored on computers?
  - How much and what information needs to be shared?
  - Will the computers be networked?
  - Is work done from home or from an office?
- How often will this technology be used?
- What work will be done in-house?
- What will be outsourced, if any?

What are the areas about which I know little? How much time would I waste trying to figure out how to do something about which I am unsure? (Many businesses like to outsource the payroll and withholding process.)

- What is the cost-effectiveness of outsourcing?
  - If I know the area well, can I do the job more cheaply myself?
  - If someone has much greater knowledge than I do, shouldn't I just pay someone who can do it quickly and accurately?

How much time would it take for employees or me to learn the technology? Is it more cost effective to outsource?

- Do I need a database to keep track of customers/clients?
- How much financial tracking will be done in-house?
- What kind of information will my business need to keep on file/computer?
- What type of technology will my business need to handle the work?
  - Computers
  - Printers
  - Copiers
  - Faxes
  - Scanners
  - Cell phones/pagers
  - Walkie talkies

Rule of Thumb:
Technology that is purchased by the company is the property of the company. Treat it as such.

What should I think about when considering technology costs?

Getting carried away with buying all the latest technology equipment is easy to do. Be sure that your technology purchases are included in your start-up costs, and **stick to the budget**. Avoid purchasing anything you do not need.

Be sure to research costs with various companies and types of equipment. Costs often vary greatly.

How soon will the technology be outdated and need to be replaced? If a piece of equipment is extremely cheap, find out how long it will be usable.

Make sure your equipment matches your business needs. Do I have enough bells and whistles, or do I have too many?

Rule of Thumb:
Most of us love the new technology "toys," but watch out for overdoing it. Purchase only what you know the business will use.

Legal Issues

- Pay attention to licensing agreements for all software.
- If you have employees, do you have an appropriate and acceptable technology use policy in place? As the employer who owns the equipment and software, you are responsible for anything an employee does on that computer. In other words, if an employee goes to inappropriate websites, you may be held responsible. Most companies make sure that the use policy includes termination of the employee for inappropriate use of technology.
- Make sure that employees understand your company's use policy regarding technology. Have them sign an acknowledgement form stating that they have read and understood the use policy.
- Software must be purchased, not copied from someone else's computer. The copyright laws are clear about pirating software. Make sure that you register your software when it is installed on your computer.
- Be sure that employees know up front (i.e., when they are hired) that all computer activities may be monitored by the business owner(s) or manager(s). This issue has repeatedly been taken to court, and the employees always lose the argument. If the

boss says no surfing the net while on the job or no wasting time e-mailing friends from work, then the employees are not to engage in those activities. The company purchased the computers and the software and also pays for the Internet access. Employees are paid by the company to perform a specific job, not surf the net, e-mail friends, forward jokes, etc. Be sure they understand the ramifications of engaging in anything that could be construed as pornography on the Internet or through e-mail.

Chapter 4
Administration & Management:
What if I've never managed a staff before?
Do I need to know everything?

You most likely already have at least some administrative and management skills. You just may be unaware of them. Always look to your life experiences, including volunteer activities and everyday interactions, to get a good idea of what your management, people, team, and administrative skills may be.

When you look at all the activities you have done throughout your life, you will discover that you have more skills and knowledge than you may have realized.

Rule of Thumb:
You don't have to be an expert in all areas. Finding the right expert to complete a task is the mark of a good leader.

How do I determine what skills and knowledge I already have?

Have you ever been part of a sports team or played in a musical group? Have you ever organized or helped organize a family reunion or other event? How about organizing and managing a birthday party for ten or fifteen 8-year-olds kids? Did you coach little league? Have you taught a youth or children's class (e.g., Sunday School, Saturday School) at your church, synagogue, or other faith organization? Those experiences give you team, leadership, and management skills.

Rule of Thumb:
Look at your life experiences and everyday activities and skills to discover what business know-how you already have. You most likely know more than you thought you did.

Do you figure out a monthly household budget – how much money you have coming in, and how much may be spent on what each month? Yes, we all must do that. Knowing how to manage your household budget, whether large or small, gives you the basics you need to know about handling money in a business. Budgeting your home expenses, paying your monthly bills, balancing your check book, knowing when to say "no" and when to say "yes" to spending – all those give you some basics for administrative management of business finances. Most businesses have at least a ballpark idea of what the monthly gross income will be and what the monthly expenses are. If the expenses outstrip the income, some adjustments need to be made – just like at home. You have the skills – just transfer them to the business setting.

How do you work out differing points of view with your family or friends? Successfully resolving problems with friends and family means that you have useful people skills. Are you a parent? Do you run a household? How about just keeping your family organized on a day-to-day basis? Management and leadership skills go with parenting and running a home. Again, just transfer those skills to a business setting.

How do you budget time among work, family/ home, and relaxation? We all need to make time outside of work for family, friends and relaxation activities. Time management at work isn't so different. How much time do you need for each task, and what has to be done first? How many hours each week to you need to deal directly with customers? How much for record keeping? How much for communication (e-mails, letters, phone calls, memos, etc.) with customers/clients, suppliers and employees? Do staff meetings need to be scheduled? If so, how much time will each meeting take? How often will meetings need to be held? How much time might you need to help employees with problems or their time management?

Managing your work sometimes becomes much easier when you've been doing it a while. Always be willing to make changes that will help the business run more smoothly. Reassign tasks to those who can best handle them.

Rule of Thumb:
If you need to acquire or sharpen a skill, look for free or inexpensive online or community workshops and classes.

What are some of the basics I need to know?

- Record keeping
  Receipts for purchases

  Invoices for fees charged or for sales

  Balancing books regularly (at least monthly, but more often is preferable; some businesses do it daily or weekly; you must decide what works best for your business – but the more often, the better)

  Employee job performance (personnel files for employees)

  Customer/client information (purchases, services, preferences, etc.)

Training

- who has been trained on what and when
- what additional training is needed and by whom

Backup system for all records: hard copy and/ or electronic backup (on site or off site)

- Payroll

  Determine a convenient pay period for your company (weekly, bi-weekly, monthly)

  Decide whether or not to outsource this task: Many companies are available to do this for a reasonable fee.

  Schedule pay periods to correlate with cash flow

- Time management

  Outsourcing: What can be done more quickly and accurately by experts? Always consider outsourcing tasks that require expertise that you may not have. For instance, you will most likely hire a tax professional to prepare your business tax return.

  Oversight of outsourced tasks

  Managing staff

  Overseeing in-house tasks

  Consideration of hiring an administrative assistant

- Policies and procedures
  Vacation

  Sick leave

  Absenteeism

  Computer use

  Official spokesperson for the business

  Complaint/grievance procedures

  Special request by employees (extended time off, change in job duties, etc.)

Make sure that you have policies in place for all of the above issues. Inform employees of these policies when they are hired. Again, having them sign a form indicating that they have read and understood the policies is a good practice.

> **Rule of Thumb:**
> Know your strengths and weaknesses. Concentrate on and develop the strengths; outsource the weaknesses or assign them to an employee who is strong in that area.

Why do I need to keep accurate records?

- Customer/client questions or complaints: Having the purchase dates of goods or services, what was done, who was involved, etc., may be critical to resolving any problems.

- Employee records: time on the job, current salary levels, payroll, job performance, absentee record, etc.
- Tax purposes (federal, state, and local)
  ALL financial transactions need to be recorded so that you have accurate information for the tax return.

All income must be reported.

All allowable deductions should be taken. Don't miss taking an allowable deduction just because you can't find a record or the receipt.

Maintain records for at least five (5) to seven (7) years in case of an IRS audit.

Rule of Thumb:
Outsourcing does not equal ignoring. Maintain oversight over every task that is outsourced.

Do I need to be an expert in everything?

Make sure you know the areas at which you are the best. If you are extremely good at dealing with unhappy customers, do that yourself. If you are weak in writing letters to customers or suppliers, hire a company or an administrative assistant who does that task well. How are your marketing skills? You may want to outsource advertising materials to a marketing company.

Outsourcing does not equal ignoring. Make sure you know enough about all areas so that you can maintain oversight. If you hire a company to do the payroll, you need to know how the total amount of pay was figured, how the amount of withholding was determined, etc. Even though an area may not be your greatest strength, be sure to learn enough about it to know if it's being done correctly by the person or company that is doing it.

Don't waste time trying to become an expert in a weak area. This decision goes for your employees also. A Gallup study of over two million people shows that "each person's greatest potential for growth is in the area of his or her greatest strength." (Buckingham and Clifton). Consider for instance someone who has no musical talent compared to a person who has a great amount of musical talent. How much will one year of weekly lessons and two hours of daily practice help the person with little talent? How much will the same lessons and practice help the person with a great amount of musical talent? Or think of talented and not-so-talented athletes. What does daily training and practice do for each of them? 'Nough said?

Rule of Thumb:
Always show appreciation for your employees. Thank them for a job well done.

How do I manage employees?

You should know the laws related to hiring, firing, employee rights, etc. Check with a human resource expert or lawyer who can provide you with the necessary information.

Have policies and procedure in place before you hire the first person and review all policies and procedures with new employees. Have them sign a form indicating that they reviewed and understood the policies and procedures.

Remember the Golden Rule. NEVER treat an employee in a way that you would not like to be treated. ALWAYS think about how you would like to be treated.

Discuss negative issues in private with the employee. Always try to put even the negative information in positive terms. Instead of saying "I don't like how you did that," say something like "I see why you did it that way, but I'd prefer you do it this way." Avoid sounding angry. Stop, count to twenty, take a deep breath, or go home and sleep on it before getting angry with an employee (or a customer, for that matter).

Give praise. Tell your employees that they are doing good jobs. You can always say something like, "I really liked the way you did this. But, you know, when you do this other task, maybe doing it this way instead might work better."

Cautionary note: If you have a habit of resolving disagreements by yelling or barking orders at people, you will need to form a new habit, one of discussing problems to resolve them and delivering decisions and information in a calm, friendly and non-threatening way. You might consider contacting a conflict-resolution specialist at a local university or college to help you learn how to manage conflict.

> *Rule of Thumb:*
> The buck stops with you. If you're the boss/owner, make sure that you understand that you are legally responsible for the actions of your employees. Policies and procedures MUST be in place before you hire.

Legal Issues

Accurate records are necessary in the event of an IRS audit. Keep accurate records, and keep them for at least five to seven years. If you took a deduction on your business tax return but cannot prove it with valid receipts, the IRS will discount the deduction. You may end up owing taxes you had not planned on.

You are legally responsible for what your company does and what your employees do as representatives of the company. If an employee makes a promise to a customer, especially in writing, the company may be obligated to fulfill that promise, whether you, as the owner or boss, okayed that or not.

Chapter 5
Communication Skills:
How can I improve the way I communicate?

In the business world, communicating well is extremely important. If you look at job postings, you will note that the vast majority list good or excellent written and oral communication skills as a requirement for the job. You don't need – or want – to sound like a Harvard PhD English professor, but you do want to sound as if you at least remember your junior high grammar and composition lessons, as well as your high school speech class lessons.

Good communication is a reflection of the company. Spelling and grammar DO count. Have you ever received a marketing letter that was so poorly written that you simply tossed it in the trash? Most of us have had that experience. You don't want your communications to be the ones going in the trash.

What is meant by "written communication" and "oral communication?"

Written communication is anything that is written on paper, on the Internet, in e-mail, marketing/

advertising materials, etc. In other words, it is something that the receiver must read.

Oral communication is any exchange of words and information that is spoken. It can be a casual conversation or an exchange of company information on the job or at a company meeting. Oral communication is usually less formal than written communication – unless, of course, you are giving a formal presentation to a large group at a conference, meeting, etc.

Rule of Thumb:
Spelling, grammar and sentence structure (meaning complete sentences) really DO count. Written material of any type is a reflection of the company. Keep a good image by communicating well.

What are the benefits of communicating well?

- Customers will clearly understand what you are providing and for how much; good communication minimizes confusion or misunderstanding.
- Employees will know exactly what you want or need.
- Your company's image will be positive.
- Your values and your company's values will be communicated clearly, adding to the positive image of your company.

- Negotiations with suppliers, business associates and employees will be clear.
- Good communication skills automatically lead people to think you are an expert in your field. The opposite, unfortunately and sadly, is quite often true for poor communication skills: people will mistake poor communication skills for ignorance.

What about some tips to help me write better?

Clear and concise (short and to the point) is the essence of good communication. Avoid using unnecessary or extra words. Use simple, everyday words instead of long, complicated ones. Remember that business writing is about being clear and concise, not fancy.

Start writing your sentences with only the simple subject and simple verb. You can add descriptive words and phrases once you've decided what the subject and verb need to be. For instance, "Jan wrote." Wrote what? "Jan wrote the revised policy." Policy for what? "Jan wrote the revised employee policy regarding requests for vacation time." This simple writing process is used by professional writers. Making use of it will help you improve your writing. The more you practice this process, the better your writing will become.

> **Rule of Thumb:**
> Longer is not better. In good communication, excessive wordiness is not desired. Keep it simple, concise and clear. Avoid using unneeded words and phrases. People want to read information quickly.

In most cases, state the main point first. Then provide explanation if necessary. The exception to this approach is if you need to deliver some bad news. In that case, explaining the reasons first and then stating the main point may work better than stating the bad news first. An instance of this might be informing employees that no salary increases will be coming in the next year. Explaining the reasons (e.g., slow business, poor economy, etc.) first and then letting the employees know that there will be no raises may be a good way to deliver bad news. Knowing who will be getting the bad news will help you decide. How will that person (or those people) react? Use your judgment to decide what the best way to deliver bad news is.

Organize your information. Make sure that the order makes sense. Does the information need to be chronological (time order), in order of importance (e.g., reasons for limiting vacation time), or according to topic (e.g., topics for a staff meeting). What needs to be first, then second, then third and so on?

Keep communication positive. Instead of saying "You cannot leave until 6:00 p.m." say "You may leave at 6:00 p.m." Avoid "not," "never" and "no" whenever possible. Keep in mind, though, that you will use them, depending on the situation. But as a general rule, try to avoid them when possible.

Keep a "Red Flag" list that details writing problems to which you need to pay attention. If you find yourself writing any of them, a "red flag" should go up in your head. That means you stop, look at what you've written and make sure it is correct.

Read the written material out loud. Doing so slows you down and helps you to notice errors that you would miss if you just glance over the writing with your eyes.

- Proofread three times
  - Once for content
  - Once for grammar and sentence structure (the order of the words in the sentences)
  - Once for mechanics (spelling, punctuation, capitalization)

Proofreading for one area at a time lets you to concentrate only on that area, allowing you to notice mistakes more easily.

Have someone else proofread what you have written. We see our own mistakes the least often because we know what we meant to write, and our brains tell us that is what we have written. That is not always the case, though. Others see our mistakes much more quickly than we see our own.

> **Rule of Thumb:**
> Avoid using big words. Use simple everyday words that people understand. Just use the words correctly, and use correct grammar.

What tips will help me be a better speaker/ conversationalist?

Think before you speak. Slow down. Too many people try to speak too fast, making what they say hard to understand. Remember the importance of eye contact. Avoid letting your eyes wander when speaking to a person. Look at the person directly, but avoid staring.

Avoid mumbling. Practice pronouncing words clearly if you have a mumbling problem. Hire a speech coach if you need to. It will be well worth you time and money in the long run. Customers, employees, and all people with whom you deal will appreciate clear speaking.

Be aware of body language/non-verbal communication. The non-verbal cues are far more important than the words. Items like tone of voice, pacing, facial expressions, distance from the speaker, arm and hand gestures, etc., are extremely important. Read a book or take a class on communication skills if this is an area that you need to improve.

As a general rule, avoid slang in the business world. Many people many not be familiar with the slang expressions.

For people whose first language is not English, avoid slang at all costs. They may not understand expressions like "being on the same page" or "give me a ballpark figure." In our world of global business, and with so many workers coming from foreign countries (Japan, Russia, Korea, Sudan, Central and South America, etc.), slang expressions are not always understood. Slang expressions can cause confusion and misunderstanding. Slang expressions do not translate literally from one language to another.

Use "sign posts." Phrases such as "the next topic I want to discuss . . ." will help the listener follow what you are saying and help him/her remember the information better.

Use the person's name in conversation with him/her. If the person is someone you just met, repeating the person's name in your conversation will help you remember it. It also makes the person feel that he/she has your undivided attention.

Rule of Thumb:
Pay attention to verbs (those words that tell what the action is: run, see, go, give, sell, provide, buy, etc.). The single most noticeable grammar error is faulty subject-verb agreement. It's as simple as remembering to say "He saw" rather than "He seen."

How important is listening?

You've probably heard it said that because God gave us two ears and one mouth, they should be used in proportion. Everyone needs to listen twice as much as he/she speaks.

Listening is critical to effective communication. If someone is talking and giving out important information, but no one is listening, what's the point? Remember that communication is a two-way process. It takes both a speaker and a listener. The listener may then become the speaker in response to what the first person said. Then the first person should listen carefully.

Rule of Thumb:
Listening *effectively* is a learned skill. Anyone can learn it, just as one learns to add and subtract or to drive a car.

Listening is an activity that takes conscious effort, skill and practice to accomplish effectively. But keep in mind that it is a learned skill, and anyone can learn it. Find a teacher or a good manual on listening skills to learn effective techniques. People with no training in listening skills tend to understand only about one-fourth of a message.

The following truths about listening provide some clarification about what listening is and is not, as well as what role listening plays in effective communication.

- *Hearing and listening are completely different processes.* Hearing is an automatic physiological process, allowing people to hear sounds whether or not they plan to do so. Short of having a severe hearing impairment, people will hear a sonic boom even if they do not intend it. Listening, on the other hand, is an intentionally active mental process in which the listener makes a conscious effort to understand information being conveyed.

- *Listening does take conscious effort.* Listening is an active mental process, not a passive activity. Active listening results in some physiological changes similar to those that occur when a person is exercising.

- *Both the speaker and the listener are necessary for effective communication to take place.* Speaking is of no use if no one listens to make sure the information is understood. Effective communication requires both speaking and listening.

- *Intelligence has little to do with listening skill.* A genius can be a poor listener. In fact, some geniuses may be poor listeners because they are so busy talking about their own ideas and theories that they forget to listen to others.
- *Good hearing ability has little to do with listening ability.* A person with excellent hearing may be a poor listener, absorbing little or no information. A deaf person may be an excellent listener, even though the "listening" takes the form of watching sign language. "Listening" occurs through an active mental process.
- *Speakers cannot force listeners to pay attention.* Through good speaking skills, a person will draw and hold the attention of – and may even captivate – the listeners. Even so, the level of actual "listening" is up to the listener.
- *Listening skills are gained through learning and practicing effective listening techniques.* No one is born a good listener. The right skills must be learned and practiced. Practicing poor listening skills only results in strengthening poor listening behavior.
- *Good writers or speakers are not necessarily good listeners.* Writing and speaking skills are different from listening skills. Make the effort to learn all three.

Rule of Thumb:
Know where to find resources for checking spelling and grammar. A dictionary and a grammar book, or online resources, for help with spelling and grammar are essential.

What are some other general pointers you can give me?

Always thank people for whatever they have done. If customers come into your store just to browse, thank them for coming into the store. They may come back, especially when they recall how friendly and polite you were.

Remember the hand-written thank-you note. In this age of computer communications, the hand-written note will stand out. A note with only two or three short sentences thanking a person for a meeting, a favor, or whatever, will be remembered far longer and better than will a quick e-mail.

Ask questions for clarification if you do not understand what someone is trying to tell you. You also must always be ready to answer questions if someone has not quite understood what you have said.

Always be polite and gracious and wear a smile.

Be aware of and sharpen your networking skills – not the computer type, but the "getting to know people" kind of networking. These skills will benefit your marketing/advertising, increase business connections, and help spread the word about your business. More information on this is found in the next chapter.

Legal Issues

Information sent out by the company, in most cases, creates a binding agreement. Be careful to make sure that your writing says what you intend it to say. For instance, if you e-mail a customer promising a refund within 30 days of purchase for a product he/she wishes to return, you must give that refund if the customer returns the item within the 30 days. Otherwise, you may face a law suit. The customer has a written document (the e-mail) to prove that he/she was promised a refund.

If you are unsure about any legal issues in a written piece, especially items such as contracts and company policies, hiring a lawyer to look over the materials is well worth the time and money. Doing so could save you a great deal of both time and money – and grief – down the road.

Resources like LegalZoom.com or "Business in a Box" (software) may help you write legal documents, but be careful. Do not copy them word-for-word. Be sure to include your information accurately. Have an expert look them over.

Rule of Thumb:
Have a lawyer look over all your legal documents. Doing so may save you a great deal of money and grief later on.

Chapter 6
Marketing/PR/Sales:
How do I promote my business?

A great deal of sales and marketing is plain old common sense. Marketing a Medicare supplemental insurance policy on YouTube (a youth-oriented online site) would not be a good idea. The following items give you some important issues to think about when you are deciding how to market your product or service.

Always remember that marketing goes beyond just advertising. Marketing is an entire culture for your business, including promotion/marketing, customer service, follow-through on distributing or delivering your service or product, service after the sale, and even the appearance of your store or office.

Know your market

Identify the people who are most likely to buy your product or use your service. If you are selling lawn mowers, you would not mail marketing items to people living in apartments or condominiums. Again, marketing involves a great deal of common sense.

Do market research if needed. Sometimes market research may be as simple as sending out a survey in the mail or looking up information on the Internet.

Questionnaires given to current or prospective customers can identify possible problems, as well as new products or services that you may be able to provide. Questionnaires may be mailed out or made available in your place of business.

Pay attention to changes in population, legal developments, and local economic conditions. Having this information can help you easily identify problems and opportunities. For example, changes in health care laws will require everyone to have health insurance. Most information of this type may be found on the Internet. Your local city and state websites, as well as sites such as business.usa.gov, will provide most demographic and legal information that you may need.

Consider demographics of your target market: age, gender, education, ethnicity, geographic location, and economic status.

Rule of Thumb:
Know your market! Who will buy your product or service?

Remember the four Ps

Marketing practices have identified four areas necessary for successful marketing. These four areas make up what is generally called a "marketing mix."

All four areas begin with the letter "P" to make them easy to remember.

- **Product:** a product or service that people need or want
- **Price:** what the price of the product or service should be
- **Place:** making sure the product or service is located where people will buy it
- **Promotion:** marketing your product or service to those who are likely to purchase it

Rule of Thumb:
The four Ps are all part of a total marketing plan: Product - Price - Place - Promotion.

What are some of the marketing/PR avenues I could use?

- Television and radio
- Newspapers
- Direct mail (postcards or fliers)
- Newsletters
- E-mail (Be careful not to overdo the e-mail marketing; people get tired of what they consider spam.)
- Your business's website
- Magazine ads
- Program ads (concerts, etc.): consider a trade-off for an ad; can you supply something for the

concert's or play's needs in exchange for an ad?

- Exhibiting at a trade show
- Seminars: go to them; put them on
- Writing articles for a publication that centers on your product or service
- Donating products or services to a non-profit in exchange for acknowledgement of your contribution (in a printed program, on a poster, on a flier, etc.)

Rule of Thumb:
Marketing does not need to be expensive. Determine which marketing avenues work best for your business. Get cost estimates and determine what will likely reach the most potential customers for the lowest cost.

How will I know if my marketing is working?

- Measure clicks on your website and the resulting sales.
- Consider conducting surveys. Survey Monkey is an easy online way to conduct a survey.
- Ask your clients/customers for feedback. Asking them to complete a simple evaluation form or comment card can be extremely helpful.
- Avoid continuing to pay for marketing that doesn't work. For example, running ads in

an expensive magazine that may result in only one or no purchases is not cost-effective. Find the marketing outlets that work for your business and target market.

Networking: Is it helpful? Do I need to do it?

Never underestimate the power of networking. According to many recruiting experts, networking accounts for most jobs found in today's employment market (Guffey). The same networking skills one may use to find a job may be used to create business contacts. But remember, it's about building relationships, not about handing out as many business cards as you can carry.

The following tips may help you build business relationships, which may then help you build your business.

- Join professional organizations related to your business.
- Attend events sponsored by your professional organization.
- Listen: Plan to listen 80% of the time.
- Always be considerate and polite.
- Join your local chamber of commerce.
- Attend events, especially networking events, sponsored by your chamber of commerce or other professional associations.
- Learn to introduce yourself. Yes, you can learn to walk into a room full of strangers and strike

up a conversation.

- Ask questions of the people you run into at networking events. Most people enjoy telling you about themselves. However, avoid asking personal questions (for instance, about family) until you know the person better.
- Keep in mind some stand-by questions you might use to strike up a conversation with someone you've just met.
  - How long have you been with your company/business?
  - What brought you to that company?
  - What all does your job entail?
  - Tell me a little more about your company/business?
  - Are you originally from this area?
  - How did you get interested in this field?

Stay in contact. Relationships are built through continuing contact. Avoid contacting the person only when you need something.

Follow up with the new acquaintance soon after you meet. Studies show that most people fail to follow up, resulting in the loss of the relationship. The follow-up may be as simple as an e-mail saying that you enjoyed meeting him/her.

Remember the power of the hand-written note. If you meet someone that you believe may be helpful to your business in some way, send that person a short thank-you note, saying how much you enjoyed meeting him/her and that you look forward to seeing him/her again.

Rule of Thumb:
Always plan to listen 80% of the time; plan to talk 20% of the time. Listen to your customers/clients.

Legal Issues

Be aware of the truth-in-advertising laws. While we all want to present our products or services in the best way possible, avoid promising something that cannot be delivered. Avoid making product claims that you cannot prove.

Chapter 7
Human Resources (HR):
How do I go about hiring employees and managing them once I hire them?

Employees can be the greatest resource your business has. Hiring and keeping good employees is critical to the success of your business.

What are Human Resources?

Human Resources, usually referred to as HR, deals with hiring, firing, job performance records and evaluations, and legal issues involved in employing people. Legal issues and employee rights make some of the issues a bit more involved than they were many years ago. With the needed information, you can build good relationships with your employees while making sure that you meet all legal requirements.

Rule of Thumb:
Make sure you know all the legal requirements of being an employer, from hire to fire, including employee rights.

How do I know when to hire a new employee?

- The work is too much for me to handle; I can't continue working 70-80 hours each week.
- The work is too much for my current employee(s) to handle without putting in a large amount of overtime.
- Additional expertise is needed in a specific area (e.g., accounting, payroll).
- Ask yourself some important questions.
  ○ Will the new hire benefit or hurt my business's bottom line in the long run?
  ○ Will the position be part-time or full time?
  ○ Will I need this person long-term? If not, should I hire someone on a temporary basis?
  ○ Will I provide benefits like health insurance and a retirement plan?

What needs to be in place before I can hire someone?

- Employee Identification Number (EIN): information for applying online, by phone or by fax is found on the Internal Revenue Service website (irs.gov)
- Legal requirements
  ○ Set up records for withholding income and other taxes.
  ○ Have employee(s) fill out form I-9 (Employee Eligibility Verification).
  ○ Have employee(s) fill out W-4 (income tax

withholding information).

- ○ Register with your state for state tax withholding.
- ○ Secure workers compensation insurance.
- ○ Register for unemployment insurance tax with your state.
- ○ Check with your state to see if disability insurance is required; if required, make sure you have a payment process in place.
- ○ Display required posters in the workplace: Hourly minimum wage and Safety & Health requirements (for more information go to business.usa.gov and type in "workplace posters").
- ○ Have a non-discrimination policy in place.
- ○ Set up policies and procedures, such as the following:
  - Absentee/vacation/sick leave policy
  - Family leave policy (maternity, paternity, family illness, etc.)
  - Procedure for job performance evaluation
  - Grievance/complaint policy
  - Non-discrimination policy
- ○ Job description
  - Specific job tasks (what the person needs to do on a daily basis)
  - Days and hours to be worked
  - Education requirements

- Skill requirements
- Experience requirements

Even though you may not include the pay/salary in the job posting, you need to know how much you are willing to pay.

Where do I post the job opening to find the right employee?

Here is a short list of places where you can start looking for employees:

- Your website
- Online career sites, like monster.com
- Local newspapers (both hard copy and online)
- Trade publications
- Professional organizations to which you belong
- Career centers at local high schools, colleges and universities
- Networking through business associates and acquaintances

Rule of Thumb:
Post the job opening only in places where people who have the right skills would be looking for a job opening.

How do I know the right person to hire?

Write a job opening description. List all necessary job qualifications, hours and days to be worked, responsibilities and duties, and how the job fits into the business as a whole.

Check out the résumés and cover letters/letters of application.

- Does the résumé include all the needed qualifications (e.g., education, training, experience)?
- Do the résumé and cover letter include the information you need to decide if you want to interview him/her (e.g., qualifications, skills, etc.)?
- Eliminate résumés that do not have the required qualifications.

Consider testing the person's skills required for the job.

Prepare sample interview questions, such as the following:

- How did you hear about his job?
- Tell me how your past experiences have prepared you for this job.
- In the past, what has kept you interested in a job?
- Tell me about your educational background.
- What experience do you have in this field?
- Tell me about a time you helped a company run better.

- Tell me about a problem you had at another job and how you handled it.
- What is your greatest workplace success so far?

Avoid asking inappropriate/illegal questions like the following:
- How old are you?
- Are you married?
- Do you have children?
- How much do you weigh?

Check applicants' references.

Make the job offer you think will be best for your business.
- For a full-time position, base the offer on continued good job performance (check your state's employment laws; some states allow firing for any reason within 90 days of hire).
- For a part-time position, determine if the job will remain as part-time, be temporary, or expand to full-time.
- Agree on hours, salary, and benefits.
- Determine start date.

Should I hire family members or friends?

Hiring family members or friends can be extremely tricky. A family member may want to work in your business but may not have the needed skills. Weigh the pros and cons VERY carefully. Be aware that disagreements could strain relationships with these family members or friends.

Legal Issues

Be aware of questions you cannot legally ask in an interview. Stay away from questions that involve the following:

- Religion
- Age
- Ethnicity
- Cultural background
- Sexual orientation
- Marital status
- Political views
- Family situation (e.g., How many children to you have?)
- Health issues that would not affect the job

Always check with your local, state and federal governments to make sure you are meeting all legal requirements for having employees.

Rule of Thumb:
Make sure you know what questions cannot legally be asked in an interview. Keep yourself out of possible legal trouble.

Afterword:
Some Final Thoughts on Conquering the Basics

As you can see from the information in *Rule of Thumb: A Guide to Small Business Basics*, starting and running a business takes a bit of know-how. The information in this book gives you the basic steps you must follow to start a business, as well as information needed to help you keep your business running.

As a business owner, you will need to keep a number of facts in mind. The following are reminders of some basic information, of which you may need to remind yourself when the going gets a bit tough.

- Starting and running a business takes a great amount of planning, care, attention, time and hard work.
- Owning a business involves making important financial decisions. Consult a professional when needed.
- Starting and running a business requires filling out and filing a number of legal documents.
- Be prepared to make financial sacrifices, especially when you first start your business.
- Being in business for yourself is not a 40-hour-

a-week, Monday-through-Friday job. Be prepared to put in many long hours, especially in the beginning or as your business grows.

- A positive attitude and a stick-to-it outlook are critical to the success of any business. Attitudes will show in your actions and your face, whether you think they do or not.
- Always ask for help right away when you need it. Do not wait until it's too late and your business is in serious trouble.

When you need additional answers that are not in this book, take the time and effort to find resources that will answer your questions (check the list of resources at the end of the book). The authors of this book wish you great success in all your business endeavors. Take the information that *Rule of Thumb: A Guide to Small Business Basics* offers you, apply it, and get started on building your successful business.

Business Resources for Small Business Owners

legalzoom.com	Online access to preparing and filing legal documents
uschamber.com	United States Chamber of Commerce
SCORE	Formally Service Corps of Retired Executives

Office of the Secretary of State (check with your individual state)

State Department of Revenue (check with your individual state)

Entrepreneurship programs with local universities and community colleges

Law schools at local universities

Local Chamber of Commerce

Local business organizations

Local trade unions related to your business

Micro business loan organizations in your area

State Chamber of Commerce (check with your individual state)

References

Beal & Associates Business & Management Supersite. "Myths About Listening." http://work911.com/communication/listenmyths.htm

Brooks, William Dean, Robert W. Heath. Speech Communication, 7th Edition. Dubuque: William C. Brown, 1993.

Buckingham, Marcus, and Donald O. Clifton. Now, Discover Your Strengths. New York: The Free Press, 2001.

Canavor, Natalie, and Claire Meirowitz. The Truth About the New Rules of Business Writing. Upper Saddle River, NJ: FT Press, 2010.

DeBaise, Colleen. The Wall Street Journal: Complete Small Business Guidebook. New York: Three Rivers Press, 2009.

Guffey, Mary Ellen, and Dana Loewy. Business Communication: Process & Product, 7th Edition. Mason, OH: South-Western, Cengage Learning, 2011.

Leonard, Thomas. "The Top 10 Myths of Listening." <http://www.coachville.com>, 2003.

Nickels, William G., James M. McHugh, Susan H. McHugh. Understanding Business, 8th Edition. Boston: McGraw-Hill/Irwin, 2008.

Business link to U.S. Government, <business.USA.gov>

Rule of Thumb for Business, <http://ruleofthumbbiz.com>.

United States Internal Revenue Service, <http://www.irs.gov>.

United States Small Business Administration, <http://www.sba.gov>.

About the Authors

Michael Mitilier is the Founder of the Rule of Thumb for Business book series and co-author of "Rule of Thumb: A Guide to Small Business Basics". He has over 25 year of experience in delivering, planning, and implementing training programs. Michael spent 13 years building a training and development company before being diagnosed with lymphoma in 2004. He is a survivor at all levels! That year, his love for life and others took Michael in a different direction and he decided to use his innate talents and lifelong results-oriented attitude to help nonprofits achieve their missions and goals. Michael joined the Nonprofit Association of the Midlands (NAM) as their Director of Member Services. Always looking up and beyond, he founded and led the Small Business Association of the Midlands. Michael is currently the Director of the Small Business Academy for the AIM Institute and a certified Gallup Entrepreneur Acceleration System Guide.

Contact Michael at michael@ruleofthumbbiz.org

Marian Shalander Kaiser owns WriteWorks, Inc., a consulting company providing services in editing, writing and grant writing. She also helps others improve their communication skills workshops and training in written and oral communication skills, public speaking/presentation skills, effective e-mail communication, and relationship-building skills (i.e., networking skills). She is an adjunct professor at the University of Nebraska at Omaha (UNO), teaching Managerial Communications. She also provides both the written and oral communication skills components for UNO's Executive MBA Program, Professional Management Education Program, and Nebraska Business Development Center (NBDC).

Her professional experience includes Corporate and Foundation Manager for the Omaha Performing Arts Society (Omaha, NE), Executive Director of the Bluffs Arts Council (Council Bluffs, IA), and Associate Director of the National Conference for Community and Justice (NCCJ) Midlands Region (Omaha, NE), now known as the Conference for Inclusive Communities.

Kaiser is co-author of *Rule of Thumb: A Guide to Small Business Basics* and sole author of *Rule of Thumb: A Guide to Communication Basics for Business Owners &*

Managers. These books are part of the *Rule of Thumb* series of business books produced by "Rule of Thumb for Business," an Omaha nonprofit organization providing information and resources for small business owners. Kaiser is also co-author of *Your High: Life-Changing Broadcasts from Andy Greenberg.*

Kaiser completed her undergraduate work in English and Education at the University of Nebraska at Lincoln and earned her Master of Arts degree in English from the University of Nebraska at Omaha. She holds a Certificate in Nonprofit Management from the University of Nebraska at Omaha and a Certificate in Arts Administration and Management from the University of Massachusetts at Amherst. She serves on the boards of directors of several non-profit organizations and plays violin in Orchestra Omaha, a community orchestra.

Contact Marian at mkaiser1@cox.net